Dedicated to the memory of my grandparents.
To Joseph McCarthy, whose tough Brooklyn boyhood reminded me
of Atlas's story, complete with muscle-bound photo on the beach.
To Irene McCarthy, who persuaded the navy sailor to settle in Rhode Island by dazzling
him with her roller-skating moves and who taught me that girls can do sports, too!

A big thank-you to my friends for helping me get through my constant dramas.
You're the best!

Also thanks to Marion, Sarah, and Tejal, for the help with this book.

The Story of Charles Atlas

STRONG MAN

by MEGHAN McCARTHY

Dragonfly Books ⇢ New York

Over one hundred years ago, a large steamship sailed to Ellis Island in New York Harbor. It was packed with people eager to come to America to make a better life. On board was a small boy named Angelo Siciliano. He had traveled all the way from Italy and spoke almost no English.

Although Angelo didn't know it yet, he would go on to do great things.

Angelo spent his boyhood in Brooklyn, New York. His waterfront neighborhood was filled with Irish, Jewish, Polish, and Italian immigrants. Life on the streets was TOUGH.

Because of his small size, Angelo didn't stand a chance. On his way home one night, he was badly roughed up by a neighborhood bully. "It seemed like he was beating the brains out of me," Angelo said later.

Things didn't get easier for Angelo as he got older. On one beautiful sunny day, Angelo took his date to the beach and a strong, beefy man walked up to him and kicked sand in his face. Angelo was humiliated.

Angelo wished he could do something to stop the bullies. He needed an idea.

After visiting a local museum on a neighborhood field trip, Angelo got that idea. There it was, a statue of Hercules, the most muscular man Angelo had ever seen! "Do you think a skinny kid could get like that?" he asked his teacher. His teacher suggested that he try lifting weights to grow stronger.

Angelo couldn't afford to buy
weights, so he made his own.
He used them at home every day,
but they didn't work.

Angelo was frustrated. He needed to think, so he went to his favorite thinking place—the zoo. There, he spent hours watching the animals. That's when he noticed a lion stretching. "The muscles ran around like rabbits under a rug," Angelo later remembered. And . . .

EUREKA! Angelo came up with a fitness routine. He realized that the lion was building muscles as he stretched, by pitting one muscle against another. Angelo decided to try the new method for himself.

And little by little . . .

He began to exercise . . .

He grew stronger and stronger!

ANGELO'S HARD WORK SOON PAID OFF!

His new muscles didn't go unnoticed. "You look like that statue!" his friends said. The statue was the Greek god Atlas, who was said to have held the heavens on his strong shoulders. From that day forward, Angelo Siciliano, already nicknamed Charlie, became Charles Atlas. A new name for a new body!

Atlas decided to show his new body off, so he became
a strongman at a Coney Island sideshow.

He lay on beds of nails
while a grown man stood
on his chest,

he bent iron bars into giant U's,

and he lifted heavy objects. People were amazed by his strength!

Atlas also entered the World's Most Beautiful Man Contest, and he won. A year later, he entered a body-building competition and won that too! He was crowned "The World's Most Perfectly Developed Man."

Dawn of Glory—Brooklyn, New York

Energy in Repose—Cleveland, Ohio

Alexander Hamilton—Washington, D.C.

George Washington—New York, New York

Well-known artists seemed to agree and hired Atlas to pose for over seventy-five statues that can be seen across the country to this day.

Atlas also became famous for his stunts. He once pulled
a 145,000-pound train with his bare hands!

Everyone wanted to be like Atlas, so with the help of his business partner, Charles Roman, he started a fitness course.

"Sick and tired of being soft, frail, skinny, or flabby—only feeling half alive?" Atlas asked in an advertisement. "I know just how you feel." And he did.

There was much more to Atlas's course than big muscles. "Take charge of your life!" he told his pupils.

Charles Atlas's passion for fitness was contagious.
Even his secretaries joined in the fun.

Dear Charles
I have a great
store! I put my
to work by lif
my life is so muc
I often
After
Before
JOHN MAYER
MR. CHARLE
Dept. KC
49 West
New York
Dear Sir,
I Have been fo
your course for
three months an
have been making
real progress!
Here is a

And people everywhere wanted them, too. The Atlas course sold millions of copies.

Atlas loved the many gifts his success brought him. He cherished the letters he received from fans all over the world.

Charles Atlas may have come from humble beginnings, but he was determined to succeed—and he did. He remained in great shape up until the day he died. His fitness system, called "Dynamic Tension," is still used today by people who want to get in shape.

Charles Atlas's measurements are on file as the perfect specimen of the human body. He is still considered "The World's Most Perfectly Developed Man."

TRY IT YOURSELF!

HERE ARE FOUR FUN EXERCISES YOU CAN DO TO STAY FIT.

Exercises by Tejal Asher, DPT, CSCS, and Sarah Emmanuel, PT, CYI.

SPLIT JUMP

Starting Position:
Take a big step forward. Make sure you are standing up tall like a soldier. Lower your body so that your back knee almost touches the floor.

Motion:
Push with your legs and jump up in the air as high as you can. Throw your arms up in the air at the same time like you're reaching for the sky. Land in the same position you started with.

Number:
Do 10 with the right leg in front and 10 with the left leg in front.

Starting Position:
Stand with your legs apart, holding your arms out in front of you.

Motion:
Bend your hips and knees, pushing your buttocks back like you are going to sit on a low chair. Come back up to starting position.

Number:
Do 20 times.

MINI SQUAT

PUSH-UP ON KNEES

Starting Position:
Start on your hands and knees like a dog. Walk your hands forward so that your body is straight like a board. Look in a mirror to make sure your back is straight.

Motion:
Bend only your elbows to lower your body. Try to touch your nose to the floor. Push up by straightening your arms. Keep your eyes on the floor.

Number:
Do 10 times.

DOWNWARD DOG

Starting Position:
Start on your hands and knees.

Motion:
Straighten your arms and legs, lifting your hips up into the air. Try to keep your arms and legs straight so that you look like an upside-down "V."

Number:
Hold for 15 seconds. Do 2 times.

A Note to Parents by Marion Hamilton

One of the most powerful tools we have available to assist with healthy child development is MOVEMENT. Movement experiences offer a special time to help children develop their muscles and coordinate their bodies. Research has shown that children who are physically fit are more likely to succeed in academic and artistic activities. And exercise reduces anxiety and encourages an active imagination.

Movement includes stretching, balancing, yoga, and sports. Exercise can be fun! Children who learn to balance work, rest, and play in their everyday lives develop healthy habits that will last a lifetime.

Marion Hamilton is an occupational therapist at the Northern Rhode Island Collaborative who has used a variety of movement activities with children for the past thirty years.

AUTHOR'S NOTE

When I asked my father, who grew up in the 1950s, whether he remembered the Charles Atlas ads, he replied with: "Of course . . . no one wanted to be skinny." Atlas embodied the boyhood notion of the ideal man from that era—strong and honest. And Atlas didn't just focus on outer beauty, he emphasized total physical fitness—a healthy diet, aerobic exercise, and no smoking or drinking. Atlas lived what he preached. *The New York Times*, in 1964, printed a list of the most important "happenings" for New Year's Eve. Along with a one hundred dollar champagne party, with entertainment by Judy Garland and her daughter Liza, was a listing for Atlas's modest celebration, alcohol-free. "It will feature carrot juice, and other sober sippings," the paper stated. This was Atlas's recipe for life. And his recipe was also followed by his colleagues, friends, and family—including his daughter, son, and wife, who was said to have proudly lifted the 180-pound Atlas.

I was drawn to Atlas's tale, however, not because he was a man of perfect proportions and healthy diet, but because he was a man of many firsts. He seemed to encompass so many of history's hallmarks. Atlas was among the first wave of Italian immigrants to step onto American soil. As the official Atlas web-

Copyright © 2007 by Corbis

site boasts: "On the Ellis Island website, Atlas is listed number one." Atlas also worked as a strongman at one of the first sideshows on Coney Island. And most importantly, Atlas was one of the first bodybuilders in the world, and the first to develop and package a fitness routine that did not require the use of weights or other equipment.

Atlas made an impact on so many people, from all walks of life, whether he ripped off his shirt at a dinner party in Paris to the shock and dismay of the fellow diners, or at Franklin D. Roosevelt's birthday party, where Atlas could be seen standing, mostly unclothed, next to a big cake. His clients were many, including the boxer Joe Louis, Robert Ripley (from *Ripley's Believe It or Not*), and baseball player Joe DiMaggio. Even the Indian leader Mahatma Gandhi asked for his advice. Surprised by the number of men deemed unfit for the U.S. Army during World War II, Atlas stepped in, going to training centers to encourage physical fitness and prepare the young men for battle.

Atlas's most important clients, however, were the millions of boys who wrote to him. The letters came from as far as Africa and China, but the message was the same—a barrage of thank-you's for helping them get better grades, better jobs, better lives. "My mom and dad are proud of me," one fan letter ended. On the surface, Atlas encouraged people to build muscles and stay fit, but what he did best was give kids the confidence and courage to stand up for themselves and follow their dreams. After all, Atlas himself had been a 98-pound weakling. As one of his fitness courses promised, "You'll stop being a wallflower—feel and look different. Man—you'll begin to LIVE!"

There is just one question that I've not yet found an answer to. Who really *was* Charles Atlas? His story, the facts of his life, have melded with the fiction. Even Atlas's retelling of his story changed slightly throughout the years. He'd become a real-life Paul Bunyan—all that was missing was the blue ox. But who was that man behind the image? Atlas wasn't just a muscleman—he was a husband and father. He was religious. But he lived a very private life, so private that all that remains are the idealized stories. Atlas was and is a legend. A folk hero. Perhaps that's the way he wanted it.

As Atlas remarked in response to his measurements being placed in the New York Public Library and in a hermetically sealed vault at Georgia's Oglethorpe University, "A couple of thousand years from now, when they start wondering what sort of bird was around here in the twentieth century, they can go to the library or open up that vault. And what will they find? They'll find me—Charlie Atlas!"

Copyright © 2007 by Meghan McCarthy

All rights reserved. Published in the United States by Dragonfly Books, an imprint of Random House Children's Books, a division of Random House LLC, a Penguin Random House Company, New York. Originally published in hardcover in the United States by Alfred A. Knopf, an imprint of Random House Children's Books, New York, in 2007.

Dragonfly Books with the colophon is a registered trademark of Random House LLC.
Visit us on the Web! randomhouse.com/kids
Educators and librarians, for a variety of teaching tools, visit us at RHTeachersLibrarians.com
The Library of Congress has cataloged the hardcover edition of this work as follows:
McCarthy, Meghan.
Strong man: the story of Charles Atlas / written and illustrated by Meghan McCarthy.
   p.   cm.
ISBN 978-0-375-82940-6 (trade) — ISBN 978-0-375-92940-3 (lib. bdg.) — ISBN 978-0-553-50785-0 (ebook)
1. Atlas, Charles, 1893–1972—Juvenile literature. 2. Bodybuilders—United States—Biography—Juvenile literature. 3. Strong men—United States—Biography—Juvenile literature. I. Title.
GV545.52.A84M37 2007 796.41092—dc22 [B] 2006023952
ISBN 978-0-553-11354-9 (pbk.)
MANUFACTURED IN CHINA
10 9 8 7 6 5 4 3 2 1
First Dragonfly Books Edition

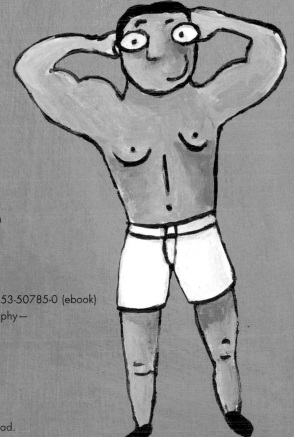